DATE DUE

DEMCO

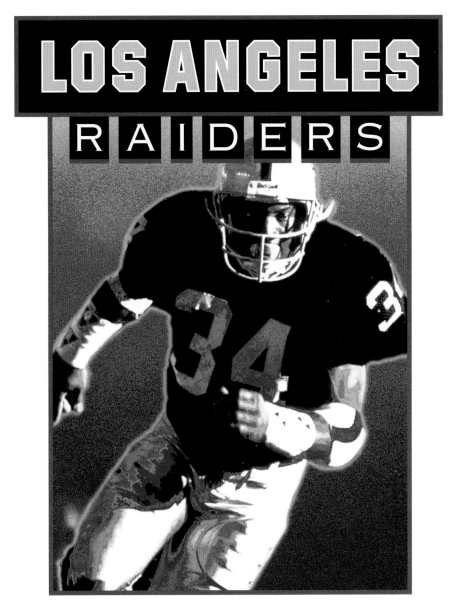

LOS ANGELES RAIDERS

Pat Ryan

C R E A T I V E ℂ E D U C A T I O N I N C .

Published by Creative Education, Inc.
123 S. Broad Street, Mankato, Minnesota 56001

Designed by Rita Marshall
Cover illustration by Lance Hidy Associates
Photos by Duomo, Spectra-Action, Wide World Photos,
Bettmann Archives, Amwest, Strictly Sports and Allsport

Library of Congress Cataloging-in-Publication Data

Ryan, Pat.
    Los Angeles Raiders/Pat Ryan.
    p.   cm.
    ISBN 0-88682-371-4
    1. Los Angeles Raiders (Football team)—History.   I. Title.
GV956.L59R93   1990
796.332′64′0979494—dc20   90-41543
                                                        CIP

In sports stores across the nation, some of the most popular T-shirts, hats, and jerseys are silver and black—the colors of the Los Angeles Raiders. From Oakland to Long Island, from Florida to Oregon, the Raiders are a team that fans support because they are winners.

The Raiders have dominated professional football since the 1960s. Not only have they been successful by pro football standards, but they also have been the winningest organization in all of pro sports for the past twenty-seven years. They lead the list with a .678 winning percentage,

Gus Otto (#34) and Dave Grayson helped make the Raiders great.

followed by the Celtics in basketball with .668, the Canadiens in hockey with .657, and the Orioles in baseball with .559 percentages.

For three decades the Raiders have defied the odds to maintain their level of excellence as professional sport's number one team. Since 1967, when the Raiders won the American Football League championship, in their very first season in the play-offs, they have been winners.

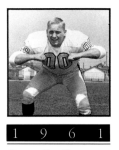

1 9 6 1

Center Jim Otto was selected to the AFL's All-League team for the second straight year.

A TRUE RAIDER

Al Davis is the man behind the numbers in the Raider organization. Mention of his name alone, provokes outbursts of emotion. The feelings may be love or hate, but even his enemies admire his tough spirit and determination. Al Davis is as tenacious in the front office as his teams are on the field. Despite what is said about him by management, Davis has earned the respect of the players.

Al Davis began his professional football career with the San Diego Chargers. At San Diego, he developed one of the most feared passing attacks in football. But while the skies were full of footballs in San Diego, the skies in Oakland were full of rain clouds.

The Oakland Raiders were the eighth and last club to get a franchise in the AFL, and they were left virtually starving for talent. Coach Eddie Erdelatz was said to have had three teams: one going, one coming, and one already there. Some players would join the Raiders early in the week and be gone by Saturday. One player, however, who stayed in camp became a Raider legend. His name was Jim Otto, but many people remember him more by his number—00.

Jim Plunkett (#16) and Kenny King (#33) carried on the Raider tradition.

Coach Al Davis guided the Raiders to more victories than in the previous two years combined.

One of the first to report at the initial Raiders' camp in Santa Cruz, Otto was a leader from day one. The six-feet two-inch, 255-pound center had played college ball for the University of Miami. Some of the established NFL players couldn't understand why such a talented individual signed with an AFL team. "I could make some NFL clubs I know," said Otto, "but it's more of an honor and distinction to be an original member of a brand new league. That's why I chose to play with the Oakland Raiders." There wasn't much in the way of honor in the first few years for Otto. The Raiders lost twenty-five out of twenty-eight games in 1961 and 1962, and players and fans alike were searching for answers.

The Raiders needed some inspiration, and they got it in thirty-three-year-old Al Davis. Davis entered the Oakland organization with a flurry of energy and new ideas. "Poise is the secret," Davis told his team. "No matter what the scoreboard says, keep your poise." In his first season (1963), the Raiders shot up to a 10-4 record, narrowly missing the AFL's championship play-offs.

The owners of the other teams in the AFL took notice of Davis's winning attitude. The new league had been battling the NFL for the loyalties of fans throughout the country. In an attempt to give their effort a needed boost, the team owners, in April of 1966, put Davis in charge of the league.

Just eight weeks later, when the two major leagues put an end to their six-year war, Davis was acclaimed nationally as the driving force who brought them together. When the historic NFL-AFL merger was completed, Davis resigned his post as AFL commissioner and began his next crusade, to bring the world championship to Oakland.

A COMMITMENT TO EXCELLENCE

Fred Biletnikoff led the club with sixty-one receptions and over a thousand yards.

With the leagues united, a true champion could be crowned, and the Raiders wanted to establish their superiority. On January 14, 1968, in the first NFL-AFL Super Bowl, the Silver and Black got their chance against the mighty Green Bay Packers, coached by the legendary Vince Lombardi.

"Seven years ago, I thought this day would never come," said Jim Otto. "We are in the Super Bowl." Other teams that had been in the league for decades hadn't accomplished what the Raiders had achieved in just a few years —all of this from a team that started playing its games on a high school field.

In the Super Bowl, Raider coach John Rauch, who had taken over for Davis when he became general manager, tried several attacks, but the young Raiders were no match for the veteran Packers. The game ended up 33-14 in favor of the Pack.

Three years after their first Super Bowl appearance the sixties would come to an end with the Raiders firmly established as one of the best teams in pro football. The strong showing came from efforts by Fred Biletnikoff, Willie Brown, George Atkinson, and Daryle Lamonica among others. The decade began with the Raiders losing. In 1961

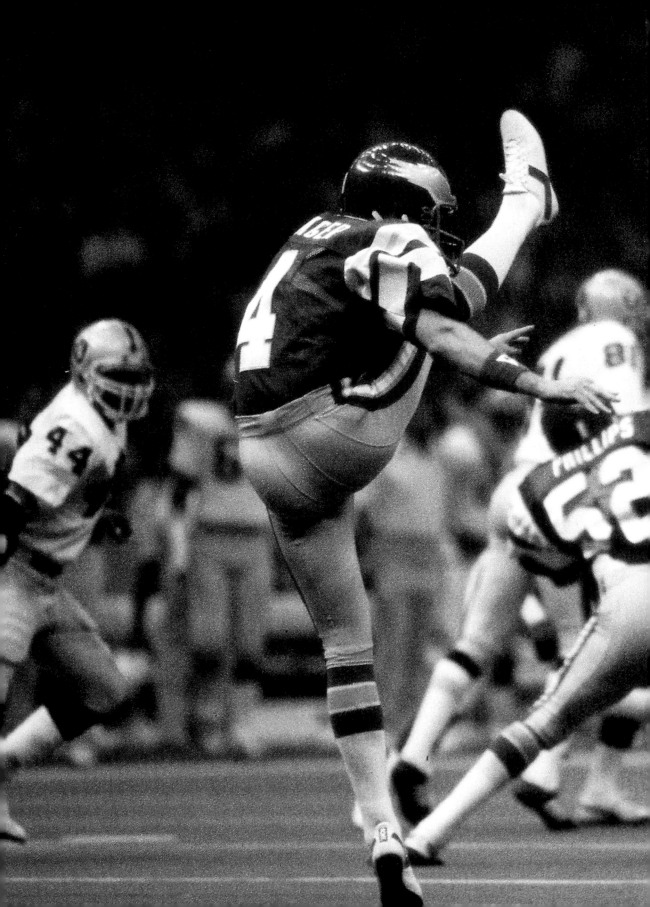

Under coach John Madden, the Raiders advanced to the conference championship game.

their record was 2-12. By 1969, however, times had changed. The Oakland Raiders finished the decade with an incredible mark of 12-1-1.

The Raiders continued their dominance into their second decade. The seventies brought a new era to the Raiders in the burly shape of a man who would rewrite the book on what a football coach was supposed to be like.

Traditionally, coaches had been strong disciplinarians who treated players as if they were animals. John Madden changed all of that with his emotional approach. "I had a philosophy," explained Madden. "First of all I really liked my players. I liked them as people, above and beyond the player-coach relationship. Second, I made a point to talk to each player personally every day. I think that's important. Sometimes there was really nothing to say—'How you doing, how's the weather, how's the wife, how's the baby?'—but at least the lines of communication were open." Madden brought fun to the game.

"I think some coaches get hung up on power or some doggone thing," continued Madden. "They forget that football is still a game of people and it's supposed to be fun. You can be intense and competitive and all that, but try to remember to laugh and have fun. It's just a football game; it's not brain surgery or World War III."

Madden instilled his philosophy in his teams, and not only did they have fun but they won as well. Madden's teams had a way of snatching victories in unusual ways, with unusual players. Typical of this was the Raiders' strong left-handed quarterback, Kenny "the Snake" Stabler.

Ken Stabler got his nickname in high school after he had zigzagged across the entire field like a snake, running a punt back for a touchdown. Stabler grew up in football country—Foley, Alabama—and played quarterback for Bear Bryant at the University of Alabama.

As the Raiders' quarterback, Stabler's greatest asset was his quick release. In his first year at the helm, he led the league in passing. Behind Stabler's efforts Oakland continued to be the team to beat. In 1972 their record was 10-3-1 and were seconds away from beating Pittsburgh when Franco Harris pulled off his "Immaculate Reception" to beat the Raiders 13-7 in the first round of the playoffs.

In 1973 the Raiders were back. Stabler, and a vicious defense led by Ted Hendricks, would take the Raiders to a 9-4-1 record. But this time the Raiders got sweet revenge against the Steelers when they thrashed them 33-14. Unfortunately, Don Shula's Miami Dolphins won the American Football Conference's championship game 27-10. Madden and his team just couldn't get over the last hurdle.

Three years later, Silver and Black entered the 1976 season under a cloud of controversy. Four times in four years they had reached postseason play, only to be sent home disappointed. Many football observers were hinting that the Raiders couldn't win the big game.

Al Davis gave Madden a vote of confidence, and Madden in turn put his fate in the hands of Ken Stabler. When Stabler was pressed about the Raiders' performance in past years, he remarked, "Last year don't mean beans to me. It's this year that counts." With help from receivers like Dave Casper, Cliff Branch, and Fred Biletnikoff, Stabler was ready.

In fact, the entire Oakland organization was prepared. From top to bottom the Raiders showed a commitment

1 9 7 3

Veteran kicker George Blanda led the team in scoring with one hundred points.

13

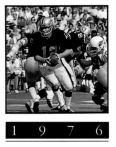

Kenny Stabler passed for twenty-seven touchdowns during the Raiders' drive to the Super Bowl.

during the 1976 season that seemed to be missing in previous years. Play after play, game after game, there was a sense of purpose in everything the team did. This dedicated effort enabled the Raiders to breeze through the regular season and their first round play-off opponent. Now, directly in front of them stood their biggest test.

The Raiders were in the AFC championship game again. Their opponents? The Pittsburgh Steelers! Three times the Black and Gold had stopped Madden's march to the Super Bowl. Would this year be any different? Indeed it would be. The Steelers should have stayed home. The Raiders turned the Steelers' Black and Gold into black and blue as they stomped them 27-7. Only one more game was needed to bring home the Super Bowl trophy.

The Raiders were finally in the locker room at the Super Bowl. Waiting for them at the end of the tunnel were the mighty Purple People Eaters, the Minnesota Vikings. Unfortunately for the Vikings, the Raiders chose that day to showcase one of their candidates for the Hall of Fame, Fred Biletnikoff.

Stabler and Biletnikoff made the afternoon miserable for the Vikings. Three of Biletnikoff's receptions set up touchdowns as the Raiders rolled to their first world championship, 34-14. After nine years of knocking at the door, it finally opened. At last, the leader that former Raider George Blanda called "the kindest and most thoughtful coach I ever had" was rewarded with his Super Bowl ring.

Madden and his team tried in vain to secure back-to-back Super Bowls, but the Denver Broncos got in the way.

Lyle Alzado earned his Super Bowl ring by crushing the Redskins.

The AFC was loaded with talent, and while Madden put strong teams on the field every year, it was difficult to stay on the very top.

THE TRADITION CONTINUES

John Madden decided that he wanted to move on and try broadcasting. He retired in 1978 with a record of 103-32-7, which included seven division titles and his victory over the Vikings. Madden didn't leave his replacement, however, with a mess. New coach Tom Flores would step in with the backing of Al Davis and smoothly carry on the Raider tradition.

Somehow over the years the Raiders got a reputation for being a haven for the misfits, the downtrodden, and the aged. When Flores took over, he had one of these outcasts sitting on the bench—Jim Plunkett.

Jim Plunkett had drifted around the league for years. He had a few good seasons with New England, but many people thought his best years were behind him. Flores saw something in Plunkett and gave him another chance. It turned out to be a terrific move as Plunkett went on to play out one of the greatest comeback stories in football history.

The Raiders had already lost three of their first five games in 1980 when Flores finally gave Plunkett the nod. Plunkett, the popular Mexican American, went on to lead the Raiders to nine wins in the next eleven games. Surprisingly, the Raiders were in the play-offs as a wild-card team.

The road to the Super Bowl is not easy for any team, but the wild-card team has to overcome playing on the road,

1 9 7 8

Sure hands: Tight end Dave Casper led the club in receptions for the third consecutive year.

A popular target of Jim Plunkett's, running back Frank Hawkins.
(page 17)

Bo Jackson created his own road in 1991. (pages 18–19)   17

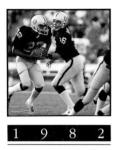

A first round draft choice, Marcus Allen was selected to play in the Pro Bowl.

as well as playing one more game than everyone else. The Raiders met the challenge, and for the first time in NFL history a wild-card team made it to the Super Bowl.

Many skeptics put the Raiders down, but Jim Plunkett and the defense, led by Lester Hayes, put the critics to rest by beating Philadelphia 27-10. Plunkett completed three touchdown passes, including a record-setting eighty-yard nuclear strike to fullback Kenny King. The Raiders had won Super Bowl XV.

The Raiders were establishing their third decade of dominance, and the best was yet to come. In the 1982 draft, Al Davis selected Marcus Allen, the Heisman Trophy winner, as their number one pick. Plunkett the veteran would soon be handing the ball off to Allen the rookie. The only question remaining, was whether or not Allen would be playing in Oakland or Los Angeles.

Al Davis and the Raider organization were torn between loyalty to the Bay Area and bigger profits. Their stadium was busting at the seams, with a seating capacity of just over 50,000. Davis wanted to put 90,000 fans in the stands, and he didn't care if they were from Oakland or Los Angeles. After a bitter fight, Davis won and the Raiders were headed south to the Los Angeles Memorial Coliseum with a seating capacity of over 90,000!

Once in Los Angeles, Davis and the Raiders would soon find out that Marcus Allen, who played his college ball at the University of Southern California, was the kind of player who would fill those seats. By the end of his rookie year, Allen had gained 697 yards. He was good for 5.7 yards every time he touched the ball. He also scored fourteen touchdowns and was the first rookie to lead the league in that category since Gale Sayers had done so with the Bears in 1965. For his efforts Marcus Allen was named Rookie of the Year, and the Raiders were headed for paydirt.

Unfortunately, Allen suffered from the sophomore jinx in his second season. A number of journalists were putting him down as a flash in the pan. But the offensive line, led by All-Pro Art Shell, knew they had a great one and it was only a matter of time before he would break loose once again.

Meanwhile, Jim Plunkett's aerial circus and the Raider defense were having the time of their lives. Al Davis was calling this edition of the Raiders one of the greatest teams to ever play the game. For Allen this only added fuel to the fire, because he wanted to be known as one of the greatest backs to ever play the game. It wouldn't take him much longer to stake his claim.

It was Super Bowl XVIII. The Raiders were trying for their third championship. In their way stood the Washington Redskins. The Redskins' defense had been ranked number one in almost every category during the regular season, and earlier in the year they had defeated the Raiders 37-35. In the earlier game, however, the Raiders were without the full services of Mr. Allen.

By the end of the game the Redskin defense was seeing a lot of Marcus Allen, but unfortunately for Washington he was running by them. At the end of the third quarter, the Raiders took over at their own twenty-six yard line. Marcus took the handoff and started to his left but was shut off by defensive back Ken Coffey. Allen leaned to his right, switched directions, and headed straight into the Redskin defensive line. "I was picking myself up off the ground,"

1 9 8 3

Passing perfection: Quarterback Jim Plunkett passed for nearly three thousand yards.

21

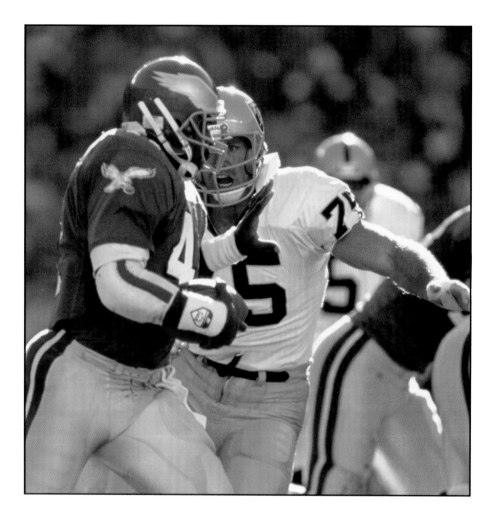

While Allen led the offense, Howie Long anchored the defense.

Raider right guard Mickey Marvin said. "Then I looked around and a rocket went through!" The rocket blasted on for a seventy-four-yard touchdown. "It was the greatest run I've ever had at this level," said Allen. Boosted by this fantastic run, the Raiders went on to post a super rout, 38-9.

Afterward an ecstatic Marcus Allen commented that, "This has to be the greatest feeling of my life. I've been to the Rose Bowl. I've won the Heisman Trophy. But nothing is sweeter than this." The Raiders' notorious owner couldn't have agreed more.

"I can say this now," said Al Davis. "I can't conceive of another team in football dominating more than this team did. This team has Ray Guy, the best punter of all time; one of the true superstar runners Marcus Allen; a fantastic placekicker, Chris Bahr; and Jim Plunkett is . . . well, if you're in a big game, Jim Plunkett is the guy you want.

"We had the best record in football over the last twenty years. We had great players and great coaches. But this is the greatest team of all."

1 9 8 4

Super scorer! Wide receiver Cliff Branch caught three touchdown passes in Super Bowl XVIII.

RAIDER PRIDE AND POISE

Greatness only comes so often. But in the Raiders' case it comes more often than others. So when things take a turn for the worse, it catches everyone by surprise. Such was the case in 1988 after the Raiders had missed the play-offs for two consecutive years.

After the retirement of coach Tom Flores, Al Davis brought in Denver Bronco assistant Mike Shanahan to re-direct the ship. It didn't work. Shanahan was released

Clockwise: Lionel Washington, Marcus Allen, Willie Gault, Bo Jackson.

halfway through the 1989 season. The fact that Shanahan was not an ex-Raider seemed to be the biggest problem—that and not winning.

Raiders seem to understand Raiders. "Once a Raider, always," says former defensive end Otis Sistrunk. "We are close. Whenever I meet a Raider today, I don't just say hello and give a handshake. I hug and kiss him."

In an attempt to recapture this feeling, Davis chose offensive-line coach Art Shell to replace Shanahan as his new head coach. Shell, who was named to the Hall of Fame in 1989, has Raider blood in his veins. Many believe he was the best offensive tackle to ever play the game. Shell went to the Pro Bowl eight times, more than any other Raider. He is one of the most respected men in all of football, and the players know they can trust him.

To win games in the NFL, however, a coach needs more than respect. He needs talent, discipline and a strong desire to be the best. One man on Shell's roster epitomizes these characteristics more than any other.

Vincent Edward Jackson was born in Bessemer, Alabama. He was the eighth of ten children and was wild as a youngster. His brothers and sisters described him as being wild as a "boarhog." The nickname "Bo" came from boarhog's abbreviated version, "bo 'hog."

Everyone knew he was a great talent. He had won the Heisman Trophy in 1985 while rushing for Auburn. The Tampa Bay Buccaneers drafted him first in 1985. Instead of riding in a limo with the Buccaneers, Jackson chose a ride in a rickety old bus to pro baseball's Kansas City Royals' farm system. A year later, Al Davis drafted Jackson

1 9 8 9

New head coach Art Shell sparked the club to seven victories in his first ten games.

A man for all seasons, Bo Jackson (right) became the Raiders most feared weapon.

in the seventh round. He was the 183rd player taken. Most observers thought Davis was crazy, thinking someone could play two professional sports.

The sports world was anxious to see if Bo could measure up. Could he survive his grueling schedule? They didn't have to wait long to find out Bo could play. In a Monday night game against Seattle, with all of America watching, Bo ran a record 221 yards, which included a breathtaking ninety-yard run. For his many accomplishments Bo was named Rookie of the Year by Football Digest. Most of the experts think Bo is just getting tuned up.

The future for Bo Jackson as a baseball and football player is limitless. He has hit monster home runs, and defensive backs bounce off him. So far in pro ball, Bo has a career rushing average of 5.6 yards per carry. (Jim

A star from the past, All-Pro Jack Tatum. 29

Howie Long, flanked by Bill Pickel (#71) and Matt Millen (#55).

Steve Smith personifies Raider "Pride and Poise."   31

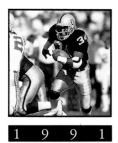

1 9 9 1

*Bo knows football!
The star back led
the club's offense
despite his
professional
baseball career.*

Brown's average was 5.2, and Gale Sayer's was 5.0.) The Raiders hope to use his talents to gain their fourth Super Bowl trophy.

The key to the Raiders' success in the nineties will be finding a leader who can work with Bo Jackson and the rest of the young Raiders. The lineup card for the Raiders is continually changing, adding new players like Tim Brown, Greg Townsend, and Scott Davis. Art Shell is said to be the kind of man who can bring the young players along and instill them with Raider pride.

Former Raider great Lyle Alzado agrees: "Being a Raider means that you perform on the field and win for Al. You give everything from the deepest part of your soul. You give your best shot. Al treats players like human beings and he'll be a part of your life forever. Art Shell is an extension of that; he's the same kind of man."

Raider fans everywhere hope this is true. If so, a return to the dominating days of the past will not be far behind. And "Pride and Poise" will once again be a Raider trademark.